THE FOUNDATIONS OF WISDOM

VOLUME 4

ETHICS STUDY GUIDE

THE FOUNDATIONS OF WISDOM

VOLUME 4

ETHICS STUDY GUIDE

FR. SEBASTIAN WALSHE, O. PRAEM.

TAN Books
Gastonia, North Carolina

Cover design by Andrew Schmalen

ISBN: 978-1-5051-2646-4

Published in the United States by
TAN Books
PO Box 269
Gastonia, NC 28053
www.TANBooks.com

Printed in India

CONTENTS

Introduction to This Study Guide

THIS IS A STUDY GUIDE to accompany volume 4 of *The Foundations of Wisdom: An Introduction to the Perennial Philosophy* (*Ethics*). In this study guide, I will explain the overall structure of volume 4 and how to read its text. I will also include essential, chapter-by-chapter questions you should be asking and answering as you read through the material. The answers to these questions are not all found explicitly in the text itself (though some are). The purpose of these questions is not only to help the student read the material carefully and to memorize or repeat information found in it but also to think about things implied by or related to the teaching in the text.

Logic, Natural Philosophy, and the Study of the Soul as Prerequisites to Ethics

If you are studying philosophy correctly, you must follow the right road, the right order of study, as you investigate each part of philosophy. This was something recognized by the greatest of the ancient philosophers, e.g., Plato and Aristotle, as well as by other great thinkers throughout the ages. St. Thomas Aquinas teaches that the study of ethics presupposes the study of natural things and the soul, which in turn presupposes the study of logic.[1] We can see the truth of this assertion in a general way even before having studied ethics in detail. For example, since ethics is about the good of man (it is the art of making a man into a good man), it is necessary to know in a distinct way what man is before determining what is good for man, just as a doctor must know what an eye is before knowing what is good for an eye. The study of the soul, and especially the human soul, provides a much more distinct knowledge of human nature and the powers and abilities of human nature that the virtues perfect. And as we have already seen from the previous study guide, the study of the soul presupposes logic and natural philosophy. So, if you have not yet studied logic, natural philosophy, and the study of the soul, you should lay this book aside and study those subjects well before taking up this book again. One way to do this is to start at the beginning of this series since the previous three volumes consider logic, natural philosophy, and the study of the soul respectively.

The Dispositions of the Student of Ethics

The fact that ethics presupposes so many other sciences naturally leads to the question: How old should someone be in order to profit from the study of ethics? Aristotle famously asserted that the young are not good students of ethics.[2] Mathematics can easily be learned by the young, and even logic and something of the natural sciences can be studied with some profit by students in their late teens. But ethics poses some particular problems for the young. Not only does ethics presuppose a

---

[1] See his *Commentary on the Book of Causes, prooemium* and his *Commentary on Aristotle's Nicomachean Ethics*, Bk. VI, lect. 7, n.17; also see his commentary on Boethius' *De Trinitate*, Part 3, q. 5, a. 1, ag. 10.

[2] See *Nicomachean Ethics*, Bk. I, ch. 3.

fundamental grasp of logic, natural philosophy, and the study of the soul, but it also requires the experience of acquiring moral habits as well as freedom from unruly emotions. Such dispositions are not usually found in the young, at least not without supernatural help. In my experience as a teacher, however, I have found that morally well-formed students in their late teens (at the end of high school or the beginning of college) do profit in some degree from the study of ethics. This is because the general principles of ethics can be grasped by students of this age and also because many of the more particular principles make sense or seem probable to morally well-formed students. Nevertheless, students of this age should be encouraged to return to the study of ethics when they advance in age, virtue, and experience.

The Need for a Teacher

In the three previous study guides, I touched upon the need for a teacher in philosophy or in any difficult matter. Ethics is no exception. There are many difficult questions raised in ethics, such as "What is happiness?" and "Is it possible for someone to become happy through his own efforts?" Since ethics is among things difficult to learn and requires much experience, it cannot be learned well simply from a book. There are so many questions that ethics raises that no book could adequately consider all of them without becoming too large. No book can answer questions the way a teacher can, and so no book, by itself, is sufficient as a guide for the life of the mind. But beyond the difficulty of the subject matter, something common to all of philosophy, there is a special reason why ethics requires a teacher. In the moral life, we need not only an intellectual guide to show us what is true but also a moral guide to give an example of how to act well in particular circumstances. The need for a moral guide is something I will take up in greater detail later. Suffice it to say, I strongly recommend that you not only read this book on ethics (together with this study guide) but also that you try to find a teacher who already knows this subject matter well and who lives according to what he knows.

The Overall Plan of the Ethics Text

After a brief introduction, the text is divided into three parts. The first part is about happiness as the target of ethics (chapters 1–4). The second part is about the means to arrive at happiness, especially virtue (chapters 5–8). The third part is about happiness as something made possible by means of acquired virtues and education (chapter 9).

The four chapters on happiness as the target of ethics begin with some nominal definitions of happiness in chapter 1, followed by a negative approach to understanding what happiness is by ruling out the usual suspects for happiness (wealth, power, pleasure, etc.) in chapter 2. Chapter 3 formulates a positive definition of happiness, beginning with the nominal definitions of happiness and arriving at an essential definition of happiness, which includes an account of the causes of happiness. Finally, chapter 4 seeks to confirm that the definition of happiness found in chapter 3 conforms to our experience.

The four chapters on the means to happiness begin with a consideration of the nature of virtue and some instructions on how to acquire and grow in virtue (chapter 5). Next, chapters 6 and 7 consider some principles and causes of the virtues, namely, choice and the other human acts that cause virtue or vice, as well as the natural law, which is the measure that reason uses to determine whether particular human actions are good or bad. Finally, chapter 8 considers friendship as a kind of perfection following from virtue and as a prerequisite to happiness.

The last chapter (chapter 9) focuses on education as a privileged road to happiness. Here, education is taken in the broad sense of leading someone to the perfection of both the intellectual and moral virtues.

The text also includes two appendices, including a list of definitions (reproduced below for the convenience of the reader) and a text that includes more detailed teaching on civic and family life.

Using Supplementary Texts

Some chapters refer the student to supplementary texts in the footnotes (and, in one case, to the appendix). These texts include the original texts of great thinkers as well as texts by modern authors. Depending upon the abilities of the teacher and students, as well as upon the time you have to complete the course, these supplementary texts can be very helpful in examining a subject in greater detail. If the teacher is very knowledgeable and familiar with the supplementary text, and the students are more advanced, these texts will be very helpful in increasing the student's knowledge of ethics. However, the course can be completed without reading the supplementary texts. They are options for those who desire to use them.

How Much Reading and Study Time Should be Devoted to Each Part?

The time needed to cover the materials in this book is the sum of the time it takes to read the book and cover the material in class. The amount of time it should take a student to read the book carefully is approximately 10–15 hours. The amount of class time to cover the contents of this book should total somewhere between 30–45 hours. So a student should expect that the total amount of time necessary to cover the entire contents of the ethics book with this accompanying study guide will be between 40 and 60 hours.

As a ballpark figure, chapters 1–4 should take approximately 15–25 hours to read and discuss; chapters 5–8 should take approximately 15–30 hours to read and discuss; and chapter 9 should take approximately 5–10 hours to read and discuss (the 10-hour estimate includes a consideration of the supplementary texts).

These are simply estimates based on my experience teaching this material. There may be reasons or circumstances why a particular student might use significantly more time than what is recommended, but it would be unusual that a student would need significantly less time than the 40 hours recommended here.

Definitions for Ethics

Ethics: The art of acting in such a way as to best achieve the ultimate purpose of human life.

Happiness (nominal): The perfect (or ultimate) good of a rational being.

Or: That good for the sake of which everything is chosen and which is never chosen for the sake of anything else.

Or: That good that totally satisfies all desires.

Happiness (essential): The activity of contemplating God by means of virtue.

Moral Virtue: A habit of choosing in the mean, according to reason and relative to us, as the prudent man would do.

Choice: A voluntary act as a result of deliberation, which determines the will to a single good means immediately within its power.

Temperance: The virtue of the concupiscible appetite that firmly inclines one to choose in the mean with regard to the pleasures of touch and taste so as to moderate the acts of nutrition and reproduction.

Fortitude: The virtue of the irascible appetite that firmly inclines one to choose in the mean with regard to fear and daring so as to strengthen one to persevere, especially in contests in which there is danger of death.

Justice: The virtue of the will that firmly inclines one to render to each person what is their due.

Prudence: Right reason about the things to be done (i.e., means to be chosen).

Art: Right reason about things to be made.

Understanding: The virtue of the mind by which the immediate and universal propositions are firmly grasped.

Science: The virtue of the mind by which the universal and necessary conclusions drawn from first, immediate propositions are firmly grasped.

Wisdom: The virtue of the mind by which one grasps the first and most universal causes of things and by which one judges all science and understanding.

Friendship: A mutual and affective love between two persons that is recognized by both and founded upon some shared good.

Pleasure: An act of an appetitive power that perfects the appetite as rest in a fitting good that is possessed.

Introduction: The Art of Living Well

Chapter 1: The Meaning of Life

What to Look for in the Introduction and Chapter 1

Try to understand the relationship between ethics and the other sciences discussed in the introduction. Also, try to understand why the first task of ethics is to find the definition of happiness and why the nominal definitions of happiness provided in the text correspond to how we use the word "happiness."

Summary of the Introduction and Chapter 1

The introduction links the previous books with this one. To this end, the introduction identifies the place of ethics within the whole body of knowledge and shows from this that ethics presupposes logic, natural philosophy, and the study of the soul to be done well.

The first chapter begins with a consideration of the ultimate aim of human choices and actions. By way of a dialogue, it manifests that the name we give to this ultimate goal is happiness. The dialogue goes on to show that the first thing we need to do in ethics is to define happiness and to determine if there is some real thing or real things corresponding to the name happiness. That is, we must begin with a nominal definition of happiness and then, if possible, arrive at an essential definition of happiness. Finally, some nominal definitions of happiness are proposed at the end of chapter 1.

Questions about the Introduction and Chapter 1

Why could someone not begin ethics without studying logic, natural philosophy, and the soul?

How is ethics different from other practical arts like logic and medicine?

Why could someone not live a good life by only aiming at proximate goods that he could get in the here and now rather than trying to determine some ultimate good like happiness?

Why would knowing what happiness is give an advantage to someone seeking to live a good life or to become happy?

Are living a good life and being happy the same thing?

Does the fact that almost everyone agrees that happiness is the ultimate thing everyone is looking for guarantee that happiness is possible for anyone?

Does the definition of happiness make clear from the beginning that every human being will find happiness in the same thing?

Why are many nominal definitions of happiness provided in the text instead of just one? Does this imply that there are many kinds of happiness?

Chapter 2: What Happiness Is Not

What to Look for in Chapter 2

Try to understand how the nominal definitions of happiness derived in chapter 1 are used throughout chapter 2 to rule out false candidates for happiness. Also, try to understand why someone might mistake happiness for the goods considered in this chapter (money, wealth, power, bodily pleasures, etc.). Finally, once the false candidates have been excluded, consider what possibilities remain for happiness.

Summary of Chapter 2

Chapter 2 considers and rejects a number of possible candidates for happiness. Since happiness, if it is possible, must be caused by some real good, this chapter considers a number of goods well-known to all and determines whether or not any of them could possibly satisfy the definitions of happiness. First, the chapter considers external goods, such as money and wealth. Next, it considers goods such as power and authority. Finally, it considers bodily goods, such as health or physical pleasure.

Questions about Chapter 2

Why begin by asking what happiness is not rather than by asking what happiness is?

____

____

____

What is the key middle term that shows that happiness cannot be some external good such as money or material possessions?

____

____

____

What three reasons are given to show that happiness cannot be power? How are these three reasons related to the nominal definitions of happiness found in chapter 1?

____

____

____

Why are goods of the body a better candidate for happiness than wealth or power?

What is the key middle term that reveals that goods of the body cannot constitute happiness?

Even if happiness does not consist of goods of the body, are they still necessary for happiness in some way?

Given that happiness does not consist in any of the goods considered in this chapter, are there any other human goods left that might be a good candidate for happiness?

Chapter 3: From a Nominal to an Essential Definition of Happiness

What to Look for in Chapter 3

Try to see how the movement from a nominal to an essential definition of happiness relies on a constant reference to experience. Try to identify the common experiences that are the ultimate foundation for the essential definition of happiness. See if you can identify the exact reasons why happiness is found essentially in one thing, which is the same for all men. Finally, try to understand how the essential definition of happiness really corresponds to human experience, even if very few people consciously pursue happiness as it is defined in this chapter.

Summary of Chapter 3

The chapter begins with the observation that, based upon the exclusion of the goods examined in chapter 2, the only candidate left for happiness seems to be some good of the soul. Next, the chapter raises and gives a preliminary answer to the question of whether happiness is found in one or many things. At this point, two methods are employed to arrive at an essential definition of happiness. The first is an inductive method, and the second is more deductive and proceeds by way of division. However, both roads arrive at the same definition and seem to confirm one another. After proposing the essential definition of happiness, some distinctions are made to clarify how happiness is in some way within us and, in some way, outside of us. Finally, the chapter returns to and solves the difficulties about the unity of happiness.

Questions about Chapter 3

Granted that happiness must be a good of the soul, why can some emotional joy or spiritual pleasure not be happiness?

What are two reasons why someone might reasonably think that happiness is found in many things?

Based upon the common experience that the great majority of men pursue happiness in different things, how could anyone reasonably hold that happiness is really found in one thing?

Is there a distinction between a conscious desire for happiness and a natural inclination for happiness?

How do the two methods of approaching the essential definition of happiness differ?

Is one method better or more certain than the other? Are both together more certain than one alone?

Do these roads to defining happiness rely upon the same experiences to arrive at their goal, or do they rely upon a completely different set of experiences?

How do the nominal definitions of happiness contribute to each road?

How do the unity and hierarchy found within human nature contribute to the conclusion that happiness is found in one thing and is the same for all men?

Why is the activity of our soul called formal happiness, while the good outside of our soul is called objective happiness?

Between objective and formal happiness, which is better and more truly called our happiness?

How can something outside of us be called our happiness?

Can formal happiness be shared by many men in common? Can objective happiness be shared by many men in common?

Chapter 4: Has Happiness Been Well Defined?

What to Look for in Chapter 4

Try to understand how the essential definition of happiness from chapter 3 in some way satisfies and, in some way, falls short of the requirements of the nominal definitions of happiness. Try to understand how the defects of human happiness possible in this life do not invalidate the definition of happiness but rather point to the possibility of a happiness that exceeds what is possible in the conditions of the present life.

Summary of Chapter 4

This chapter is for the sake of confirming that the essential definition of happiness derived in chapter 3 is a good and valid definition and corresponds to something really possible in things. To this end, the chapter raises some objections to the essential definition of happiness and attempts to answer these objections. After considering the objection that not all men seem to desire happiness as defined in chapter 3, the text goes on to consider an even more serious objection to this definition: namely, that it does not fulfill the fundamental requirements of our initial nominal definition of happiness. In response to this latter objection, the text distinguishes between the approximation to happiness possible in this life and perfect happiness, which, if it is possible, can only exist in the next life. Finally, the text speculates about what perfect happiness would look like and admits that such happiness would have to be shown to be possible by some kind of revelation and so would be the subject of theology rather than philosophy.

Questions about Chapter 4

What are the main objections to the definition of happiness provided in chapter 3?

____

____

____

____

How does desire in the sense of a natural inclination differ from desire in the sense of a conscious act of the will? Is there a sense in which desire can be "pre-conscious"?

____

____

Does it make sense to speak about "imperfect" happiness? Is happiness not, by definition, perfect?

Does the fact that perfect happiness is not possible in this life invalidate the definition of happiness?

Are there philosophical problems that philosophy cannot solve? What does this imply about the possibility of some kind of science higher than philosophy?

Why does the natural inclination for perfect happiness imply the possibility of perfect happiness?

How does the beatific vision (the unmediated grasp of what God is) satisfy both the nominal and essential definitions of happiness?

Chapter 5: Virtue: The Road to Happiness

What to Look for in Chapter 5

Try to understand the relationship between freedom, virtue, and happiness. Try to understand the different ways in which virtue, both moral and intellectual, perfect a man and make him good. Try to see the ways in which each of the particular virtues contributes to human happiness. Finally, try to understand why the acquisition of the virtues, not just knowing about them, is necessary for happiness and also requires some kind of moral guide.

Summary of Chapter 5

Chapter 5 is the longest chapter in this book, and it considers virtue as the road to happiness. The chapter begins by considering how virtue is necessary for someone to become happy. Next, the chapter argues for an essential definition of virtue. After this, the species of virtue are distinguished in general (moral and intellectual virtue) and then in particular. Before embarking upon a consideration of the particular moral virtues and the method to acquire them, the text speaks about the need for a guide in the moral life who is not just a teacher in the academic sense but is someone who gives a good example and can direct the soul in matters of particular actions. Then, the cardinal moral virtues are considered in particular, beginning with a general treatment of the passions of the soul, which are the matter of some of the moral virtues, and going on to a particular consideration of each virtue. Finally, the text lays out the method to acquire these virtues and points out that many of the principles of action needed to acquire moral virtue can only be known by habituation, which once again points to the need for the beginner to trust a moral guide in the acquisition of virtue.

Questions about Chapter 5

Why can someone not just decide to be happy without having to work at acquiring virtue?

____

____

____

What is the implied nominal definition of virtue from which an essential definition is derived?

____

____

____

Are there virtues of the body or only of the soul?

How are logic and the study of the soul used in determining the definition of virtue?

How are moral and intellectual virtues distinguished? Do they make a man good in the same way?

Explain each of the elements of the definition of moral virtue and show why each is necessary.

Why is the prudent man included in the definition of moral virtue? Why does this not involve a circular definition since prudence is a kind of virtue?

What are the species-making differences that differentiate art, prudence, understanding, science, and wisdom?

Why is a moral guide essential if someone is to acquire virtue?

How are the passions of the soul related to the moral virtues?

How is the method of going from the object to the activity used in dividing the eleven passions of the soul?

How are the cardinal moral virtues of temperance, fortitude, and justice related to happiness?

Granted that the mean in several moral virtues is not midway between the extremes but closer to one than the other, how does this affect our attempts to perform repeated actions intensely as a method of acquiring a virtue?

If some of the principles of morality are accessible only to those who have habituated themselves to certain ways of acting, does this imply that morality is purely subjective?

How can someone who does not have experience with these principles acquire virtue?

Chapter 6: Choice and Human Acts

What to Look for in Chapter 6

Try to understand how voluntary acts, especially choices, are essential for both understanding virtue and acquiring virtue. Pay attention to how the natural road from the senses into reason is used in order to establish an analogy between natural substances and human actions. Also, try to understand why it is necessary to use this analogy in order to determine whether a choice is good or bad. Finally, try to understand clearly the distinction between object, end, and circumstances and also how the principle of double effect employs each of these when evaluating a moral act.

Summary of Chapter 6

After considering the nature of virtue, the next thing to be considered is naturally the causes of virtue, especially the agent cause of virtue: good human actions. Chapter 6 begins by considering the principles of virtue, namely voluntary actions, as well as the principles of those actions that cause a voluntary act to be good or bad. After defining choice, the analogy between natural substances and human actions is used to determine what principles of choice make a choice good or bad. Just as every natural substance has a substantial form, proper accidents, and a purpose, so too every human action has an object that gives form to the act, circumstances that are the proper accidents of the act, and an end for which the act is done. If all three of these are good, then the act is morally good, while if any one of them is bad, the act is morally evil. The distinction between object, end, and circumstances is reinforced inductively by way of several examples. Finally, the so-called "principle of double effect" is explained, which allows for a moral analysis of human acts that have an intended good but a foreseen evil effect.

Questions about Chapter 6

Why is it important to consider choice in relation to virtue?

____

____

____

____

Why is choice the most important of the voluntary acts that contribute to the strengthening or weakening of moral habits?

____

What is the definition of choice?

How is the natural road at work in the determination of the goodness or badness of choices?

Why is the analogy to sensible substances necessary to determine if a human act is good or bad?

How is the object of a human act distinguished from the end of a human act? Is the end someone wills not the same as the object they will?

How is the circumstance of a human act distinguished from the object of the human act? Are some circumstances not part of the object?

Is there a difference between the object of the interior act of the will and the exterior act (for example, an act of the body) commanded by the will?

How are the five conditions of the principle of double effect related to the object, circumstances, and end of a human act?

Chapter 7: Natural Law

What to look for in Chapter 7

Try to understand why natural law should be called "law." Try to understand why following natural law makes men good and happy and why disregarding natural law makes men evil and unhappy. See if you can clearly distinguish the concepts of natural law, positive law, and the laws of physics. Finally, try to understand why man is naturally part of a larger group, such as a family and a society.

Summary of Chapter 7

Since reason and nature are the ultimate principles that are used to determine if a choice is good or bad, the next thing to consider in ethics is the practical statements (i.e., statements about what ought to be done or avoided) derived from the natural order and perceived by reason. This is nothing other than to consider natural law. Therefore, chapter 7 begins with an account of natural law and its distinction from the laws of physics and positive law. Next, chapter 7 considers the relationship between natural law and positive law.

The second part of chapter 7 considers man as naturally social: first as a natural member of a family and second as a natural member of civil society. This is a specific consideration of natural law and helps to refine the understanding of the relationship between positive law and natural law.

Questions about Chapter 7

What is the best-known kind of law?

What notion do natural, positive, and physical laws share in common? How do they differ?

In reference to what nature is natural law called natural? For example, it is in reference to natural things in general, to animal nature, to the nature of being, to the nature of squirrels, etc.

Why is natural law the standard by which positive laws are judged?

How does someone know that they should or should not act a certain way simply based on knowledge of the natural law?

Why is natural law the same everywhere and at all times? Is that true about all moral precepts?

Why is being a member of a family natural to man?

Why is being a member of civil society natural to man?

What is a good definition of civil society that clearly shows the way in which it is natural to man?

Which community is more natural, the family or the state, and why?

Since the common good always takes precedence over the private good, should the family be wholly subject to the state in all matters?

Chapter 8: Friendship

What to Look for in Chapter 8

Try to understand why friendship is a topic that ought to be considered in ethics. Try to understand how the three kinds of friendship are not friendship in the same sense of the word but are said analogously. Finally, try to understand why only a friendship of virtue deserves to be called friendship in the truest sense.

Summary of Chapter 8

This brief chapter first considers why friendship should be treated in ethics and then goes on to briefly describe the three kinds of friendship: useful, pleasant, and virtuous. These three kinds of friendship are based upon the three kinds of common goods that friends can share. Finally, the chapter concludes by identifying some marks proper to friendship.

Questions about Chapter 8

Is friendship a kind of virtue? If not, how is it related to virtue?

How essential is friendship for happiness?

Does human nature imply that virtuous men must have friends?

Why is every friendship based upon some common or shared good?

Do useful or pleasant friends love their friends for their friend's sake?

Do virtuous friends love their friends for their friend's sake?

Between pleasant and useful friendships, which is more like a friendship of virtue?

Are useful and pleasant friendships morally bad in themselves?

Can a friendship be a mixture of more than one kind of friendship?

Since friendship is so deep and essential to human happiness and flourishing, we include some points to reflect upon that are not included in the text but are worth pondering:

What do you and your best friend share?

When did this sharing happen? Has it stayed there, or has it grown as time has passed?

Do you see your best friend as "another self"? Why or why not?

What good do you bring your friend?

Have you ever seen a supposed "friendship" dissolve? What was that relationship truly based upon? Was it really, in the end, just a relationship of pleasure or utility?

In Christianity, Jesus calls us friends (see John 15). Aristotle says friendship between the gods and men would be impossible because gods and men are utterly unequal. What does the Incarnation do that allows this sort of new relationship and intimacy?

Chapter 9: Education and Wisdom (the Return to Happiness)

What to Look for in Chapter 9

Try to understand the definition of education and how it follows from this definition and a proper understanding of human nature that the best education, simply speaking, is one that ends in wisdom. Again, try to understand why an educator or teacher is necessary to reach wisdom. Finally, try to understand the necessary connection between education, virtue, and happiness.

Summary of Chapter 9

Chapter 9 begins with a definition of education, using the etymology of the word as a tool to arrive at this definition. Next, granting that there may be many kinds of education, the chapter considers what kind of education is best for man as man. Finally, the text concludes with a consideration of the need for a good education to become happy and the insufficiency of ethics to complete an education in wisdom or to lead to happiness. Thus, the book concludes by pointing to the need to continue studying higher sciences, such as metaphysics and sacred theology.

Questions about Chapter 9

Can education be defined both as a kind of acting upon by an educator and also a kind of motion in the one being educated?

Given the universal principles involved in every motion, what is implied about the educator if he is an agent acting upon the one being educated?

How does a distinct understanding of human nature contribute to the conclusion that the best education for man is one that leads to wisdom?

How does education differ from job training?

Can the conclusion that the best education is Catholic liberal education be reached by reason without faith? If not, what elements of the best kind of education can be known by reason alone?

What differentiates classical liberal education from Catholic liberal education?

General Questions for Ethics

Indicate and briefly explain how the tools acquired in logic are made use of in ethics.

Show how the conclusions and principles of natural philosophy and the study of the soul are used within the science of ethics.

Give an overall account of the principal virtues of the human soul and their mutual order. Especially attend to the order in which the virtues enable a man to achieve happiness.

How does each virtue make the soul more free to experience happiness?

What is the relationship between virtue, law, and happiness?

Why is the pursuit of happiness (or virtue) not essentially selfish?